More praise for Hotel Worthy

What are we to do with the lost, broken, failed things of our lives? How do we piece together the shards of relationships that didn't last, salvage the ghosts of our younger selves? Like a daring archeologist, the poems of *Hotel Worthy* dig [deeply] into the intimate layers of years, excavating the fossils of memory, love, loss, and family history. These poems compel us to have the courage to emerge from our past shipwrecks and embark anew. This collection is a roadmap for beginning again.
 —Ansel Elkins, author of *Blue Yodel*, winner of the 2014 Yale Series of Younger Poets

Valerie Nieman writes so intimately that I wondered if I had written her poems, and I wish I had. At the beginning of *Hotel Worthy* she releases her poems to the universe. In the prose poems her language grows so precise it is haunting. My favorite poem is "Choice of Words" in which she and her father become single in the same year. He is bereft whereas she is divorced, an act which is a "civilized/Coming apart/separated like an egg." Read this book for the surprising images folded into a remarkable journey.
 —Glenna Luschei, poet, publisher, editor, philanthropist

Hotel Worthy

HOTEL WORTHY

Poems

Valerie Nieman

Press 53
Winston-Salem

Press 53, LLC
PO Box 30314
Winston-Salem, NC 27130

First Edition

Copyright © 2015 by Valerie Nieman

All rights reserved, including the right of reproduction in whole or in part in any form except in the case of brief quotations embodied in critical articles or reviews. For permission, contact author at editor@Press53.com, or at the address above.

Cover design by Kevin Morgan Watson

Cover art, "When the Night Falls" Copyright © 2011 by Marko Nadj, used by permission of the artist.

Author photo by Jan G. Hensley

Printed on acid-free paper
ISBN 978-1-941209-18-9

*To Sarah Lindsay and Mark Smith-Soto,
who have helped each of these poems,
arriving wobbly kneed, to stand at last.*

Acknowledgments

The author would like to thank the following publications where these poems first appeared or will soon appear:

A Long and Winding Road (forthcoming anthology), "Father Showed Us the Aurora Borealis"
ABZ, "Alienation"
Appalachian Heritage, "Spandrel"
Byron Herbert Reese Poetry Prize, "Apocrypha"
Chautauqua Review, "You Don't Leave It on the Side of the Road"
Connotation Press, "Catechism," "Father Showed Us the Aurora Borealis," "Harvest," "In the Middle of Things," "Lore II: Tap's Tips," and "Watch the Sun Come Up on Your Own Life"
Flycatcher, "The Life Inside"
Ghost Fishing: An Eco-Justice Poetry Anthology (forthcoming), "Harvest"
International Poetry Review, "Second Honeymoon"
Iodine Poetry Journal, "Racial Memory" (as "Reflex")
Kestrel, "Laryngitis," and "Given Half a Chance"
North Carolina Literary Review, "A Blessing on the Tongue," "On the Beach" (forthcoming in *Southern Poetry Anthology—North Carolina*), and "Work in the Morning"
O.Henry Magazine, "Last Sweet," and "Occam's Razor"
Nazim Hikmet Poetry Prize Anthology 2013, "Approach," and "Contemporary Torso"
Solo Café, "Lore"
Southern Women's Review, "Cold" (as "Weight of Cold")
Sugar Mule, "Out of the Ordinary"
Tahoma Literary Review, "Notorious"
The Otter, "Dark Matter"
27 Views of Greensboro, "Losing Ground"
Virginia Quarterly Review and *and Love…* (anthology, Jacar Press), "Live With It"

The author gratefully acknowledges the support provided by the North Carolina Arts Council and the United Arts Council/Arts Greensboro.

Contents

1 Invoke

Release	3
Hotel Worthy	4

2 Snow

Approach	9
Father Showed Us the Aurora Borealis	10
Apocrypha	11
Fillet	12
Harvest	13
Cold	14
He Whom You Love	16
The Life Inside	18
Toute Seule	20

3 Salt

Contemporary Torso	25
Live With It	26
Rainmaker	27
The Bride Comes Home to a House Planted in a Field	29
Laryngitis	30
In the Middle of Things	31
Notorious	32
So This Is What You Wanted?	34
Second Honeymoon	35
Dark Matter	36

4 Scorch

Alienation	39
On the Beach	40
Stratigraphy	42

Out of the Ordinary	44
Choice of Words	45
Watch the Sun Come Up on Your Own Life	47
Work in the Morning	48
In War	49
Losing Ground	
Dunkard Mill Run, West Virginia: The Farm	53
Greensboro, North Carolina: The Women	54
Leawood Drive: Lilies	55
Somewhere to Go	56

5 MUCK

Lore	59
Catechism	60
Spandrel	62
The Guide: Cave Paintings at Font de Gaume	63
Racial Memory	66
Old Story	67
Lore II: Tap's Tips	68
Occam's Razor	69
Last Sweet	70
Given Half a Chance	71

6 EVOKE

A Blessing on the Tongue	
Farmer's Market	75
King Lust	76
By An(y) Other Name: King Lush	77
The Arrival of King Luscious	78
King Luscious	79
You Don't Leave It on the Side of the Road	80
About the Author	83
About the Cover Artist	85

1
Invoke

Release

Each bird is
cast to the sky

like a poor man
tosses his child to water:

lift yourself
through the blue

and swim.

Hotel Worthy

I was being so careful the new blue brush held like a pen no a knife to dagger the paint down perfectly to observe the lines to honor the edges and the teacher asks me do you believe in fairness which takes me by surprise because yes yes I do believe in fairness and justice and all equal before she adds it shows in your painting you give things equal weight why should this branch be as large and detailed as that one

The greatest way to live with honor in this world is

always dress for the blues dress blues and tennis shoes and a trunk packed with mementoes not half understood by the girl child who paged old issues of *Leatherneck* and fingered the red stripes and gold eagles and some spore of honor or such breathed in not meant, not meant at all but necessary if she was to carry the dignities of first born and only (for a while) and daddy's girl sorting nails chopping weeds and shaking hands with cold hard work to be done life long

Confidence thrives on honesty

so you must walk three miles to return six Lincoln cents and go back to the cashier and stand in line for her put-upon face the red worn off her downturned mouth to say ma'am you gave me too much change ma'am and always catch the teacher's eye doing it right am I doing it right and that would be the same refrain in sweaty sheets many years later, give it your all give it your best give it and still the sidelong glance to ask has this been seen has this been caught

The purpose of life is not to be happy. It is

to know every name of every part of the sailboat from gudgeon to headstay and the capitals of the states in their polychrome glory, the Latin names for trees the characters of Shakespeare the agricultural exports of Costa Rica, why the sea is salt, and the flight path of the Arctic tern

Better keep yourself clean and bright; you are the window through which

I am watching *Charleston WV 1932* a movie made by people button-busting proud of their bridges their baby parades their new telephone building and as the film truck rolls through the downtown there on the left is the Hotel Worthy and I realize I've been trying to check in for years but not enough hours in the day the sun marching across the sky soundless its billions of bright feet its silent army bound for the routine conflagration.

2
Snow

Approach

Arms stretched wide,
right hand to the dawn,
left toward eventual night,
I face north.

As latitude rises,
life flattens:
forest to taiga,
to tundra, to permanent ice.

Everything will have
a name of cold:
polar bear, arctic fox,
glacier flea, snowy owl.

A compass is known to stray
from true north, lured
by the earth's magnetic heart.
Now the needle swings

at the approach
of a frost spirit
from those barrens
I'll have to cross

without advice,
without a companion,
or a harness of wolf-dogs,
or good boots.

Father Showed Us the Aurora Borealis

On lawn chairs sunk
to the webbed seats in snow,

we sat bundled in blankets,
faces tilted to the unrolling scroll:

Colors of a hummingbird gorget,
parrot fish, shallow seas,

mandevilla, bougainvillea,
flametree,

tropicalities weaving
in the airless

ineffable between
earth and moon,

glories we couldn't
yet compass,

our eyes since birth
whetted against sun

on snow, a palette
of twig and bone,

knowing only north.

Apocrypha

Summer: Long days athwart the wooden arms
of the grammar school year—lightning
coiled in the westerly clouds,
smell of corn swashing towards tassel.
I was stretching out, then, too,
scraggly as a rose-of-sharon before
the flowers unfurl, common as those million
gray broken stones in the tar road.
In the five-acre field I lay down
with Grandmother's carry-to-meeting Bible,
lining my way through John's gospel
'til a swallowtail fluttered past and
I followed, turning, turning, leaving
no crumb of path through the standing hay
to wind me back to where the Book
must be.
Oh God
let me find it let me find it,
the sun of no help sliding down
toward the hills and shadows
boiling out of thunderheads
black-eyed susans a crazy pattern
daisies amidst the grass that grows
to burn in the bellies of the neighbors'
cows to make milk and meat
lilies chewed in the furnace
and the Bible a pearl
a silver coin a sheep a lost
child in that green waving
until my hands tingled
with answered prayer.

Fillet

Start in the right place
and you can manage the job efficiently:
no hacking, no false moves.

Respect this tool.
Hold it lightly in your hands
because like a prayer
it can turn on you.

White flesh unfurls
like wings; the bones
cage the worldly weight.

Harvest

Across the road from our bleak farmless farmhouse
was once another, crumpled into its cellar-stones
under an orchard of apples, pears, and plums.

We shook fruit down from summer 'til snow,
gifts from householders faltered, fizzled, ruined, dead—
trees they had planted outlasting their other works.

Greengage plums glowing on black-knotted boughs.
Bartlett pears, bruised and buzzing with yellowjackets.
Pale cheeks of Maiden Blush apples, washed crimson.
Concord grapes clustering under a crawl of vines.

Last to be gathered: Wolf River apples,
large and lopsided, not much to recommend
them until put to the fire, cored and filled with brown

sugar, butter, and cinnamon, propped
on uneven buttocks for baking. Taken from the oven,
their steam clouded kitchen windows dark with November.

When the garden was in rags, when the sun
slid toward its deepest sleep, we ate.
If we thought to thank those who had planted—
eh, well, we did not know their names.

Cold

Sweat,
breath, all so

light, snow barely falling,
a sky like down,
the silence,

accumulation
of what scarcely is
in wet wool

heavy mittens
and frozen socks,
weight from spun nothing,

insubstantial as the batt
of air and fiber plumping
the pieced quilt

now spread over the cold
child—triangles of father-shirts
and mother-skirts,

his familiar overalls,
so what burdens the boy?
Fever wheels of color?

The close ranks of stitching,
regimented ten to the inch?
Grandmothers' hands

piercing, pulling,
like cold working air into snow—
what's barely there

become heavy as
quilt piled onto quilt,
snow layered to ice:

the sweating child
hallucinates glaciers.

He Whom You Love

What else could Jesus do, with Mary and Martha,
Martha and Mary, standing outside the door and pounding
pounding pounding, *come back and live with us.*
You emerge at last, dragging your nerveless feet in the dust.

Mary and Martha drive a wedge under that door, pounding.
Each time a bit less of you comes back, your eyes unfocused,
hands trembling, your nerveless feet dragging in the dust.
They can't help it, both full of life, brimming with piss and vinegar,

unable to see that a bit less of you has come back, your unfocused
eyes asquint at the grinding sun-break they greet with shouting.
They can't help it, both brimming with piss and vinegar,
while you'd loll in the bed, if only they would let you.

At the grinding-stone of sun-break they greet with shouting,
Mary begins to talk of politics and the ways of foreign people
while you'd lull in the grave, if only they would let you.
Martha wants to knead you back into shape like a loaf of bread,

while Mary wants to talk about politics and distant people
and the way the Great Sea extends until it merges with the sky.
Martha wants to knead you like punched-down bread
dough that's rising once more, roll you in her floury arms.

You swim away to where the Great Sea merges with the sky,
But they pull you back, tumbling you through the shells and weed
like dough that's rising one more time, rolling you in floury arms,
the two of them throwing you onto the beach in the sun.

They pull you back, tumbling you through the shells and weed.
You bloat and shrink at the same time, you exhale worm-ends
as their undertow throws you onto the beach in the sun.
Each time a little less of you comes back from the depths.

You bloat and shrink at the same time, you exhale worm-ends,
you spill another spoonful of blood into the grave.
Each time a bit less of you staggers back from the depths,
but Mary and Martha, Martha and Mary, pounding at the door.

The Life Inside

He would peel the bark from
wild cherry trees,
lash it into tiny canoes

that, set adrift on our creek,
might have prowed their way
as far as town, passing

under the concrete bridge
where fish shot back and forth
across sunlight, and maybe

they kept going, just going.

He made three cuts:
two to girdle, one to free
the glossy outer bark,

damp with sap and
pliable for working.
But if I kept the boats

safe in my room,
those not put to water soon
dried, pulling apart at the seams.

As for the trees, well….

⁂

These days my father
sheds like a hickory. He grows by
shattering,

leaves showers of skin
wherever he sits,
scratches at the gray

lignified layer, rough, dead,
until the inner red shows
where he has year by year

exchanged life for life:
farmhand, infantryman,
metal-bender, artisan,

bartender, chaplain,
one by one completed
and put to the stream,

away, away.

Toute Seule

My grandmother comes around the corner
of the Dordogne farmhouse, flapping her apron
after the dogs barking *vaf vaf vaf* at a fox
among the chickens. Instead, she finds
this intruder who has emerged
from the hayfield under the strong sun.
Bonjour... a suspicious ghost, she looks past me
for the army lurking in the forest
that has sent forth this emissary,
sweating and leaning on a peeled stick.
Vous êtes toute seule?

I find some words—*Oui, je suis toute seule*—
but how do I say, *comme on dit,*
Don't you recognize me?
Why don't you shuffle forward
and embrace me as before?
She has the same chin whiskers, wispy white hair,
slumped roundness bound with Grandmother's
flowered apron. I know the bird-handled scissors
down in that pocket, and scraps of herbs.
Her dogs are barking lower now, *jappe jappe.*
They are slow and yellow,
their tongues hang out because it is
too hot, too hot
and I am *toute seule*
without guide or explanation.

"*J'ai marché dans Les Gorges d'Enfer,*"
but *dans* is not correct. Not in.
Through, along. But I cannot find the word
"*J'habite à Les Eyzies de Tayac.*"
No. "*Je reste à Les Eyzies,*"
which is not so far away, maybe no more than a few
kilometers and an eon or two. I try again,
"*Je suive le chemin en la forêt,*"
through abandoned hamlets
alike in gray stone and red tile,
but no one to properly appreciate them

or the abandoned bread ovens, or the plateau
with wheel ruts cut inches deep in the limestone—
that was a road then,
but now, deep in the sighing forest,
signs on the trees pine for *repeuplement,*
the return of the lost or those who have
found themselves in cities,
to fill the vacant farms
and breed chickens and children.

*Ou se trouve le village de Saint Cirq,
là-haut? Ou là-bas?*
Là-haut, and she lifts her hand
toward a nearby hilltop that would not
seem to hide even a small village.
Est-ce q'un bistrot—y'a-til—dans le village?
Mais oui! She stretches herself to full height,
a foot shorter than this American.
Mais oui, what town would not have a bistro?

But Saint Cirq, where the Sorcerer climbs
the ceiling of his cave like Orion,
would be, in fact, *là-bas,* down the winding
road and past a leaning stone cross,
and it had no café, not even a ram-headed
village fountain from which I might drink
to bring my heart back from the Gorges of Hell
and my grandmother's ghost
without a glimmer of recognition
shooing me off with her apron:
You do not belong here, she might have said
if she had possessed all her wits
and I could have followed the words,
your feet are too heavy on this ground.
Instead she disappeared to some hidden perch,
and her dogs, which were just farmhouse dogs,
went muttering *waouh, waouh*
back to the shade.

3
SALT

Contemporary Torso

We'll likely never meet
        the woman whose torso
        glows like a lamp on the restroom wall.

Yet her absent eyes
        seek us out, demand that we
        perceive more than the slight

pout of her belly, the incurve
        of her waist, the arched back,
        her hips flaring with fertility.

The diaphanous dive
        from her collarbone swells into breasts
        rendered in silver-leaf—

such a tenuous net
        to round the body out of space,
        her life exploding

like starlight from a point
        just beyond
        our ability to see.

Live With It

It's not my hairy body
that offends you,
but my hairy mind,

mammalian, full of heat
and snot, snuffling
from leaf to leaf

in perfect pleasure of urine
and the small dark scent
from between toes.

Rainmaker

You ride into town
raising dust, your clothes loose
on a gangster body
that's been run out
of too many towns.

You swear the thunder I hear
for hours as we talk
will bring rain,
that at your touch
the sky will thicken.

You use blue scarves
and mirrors;
your hands
work overtime.

You raise a sweat.

Your words
strike the dust
like spit on a hot stove;
thin mist rises, engenders clouds.

All my pores open,
like the invisible mouths
lipping the underside
of every leaf,
sorting damp beads into balance.

My eyes leak their blue
out the corners,
lips can't contain
the spillage of my tongue,
and that swamp,

that Everglades
matted with cypress and slick sheen—
you pause where dry land
slips down, scenting storm,
wondering why this has never happened before.

The Bride Comes Home to a House Planted in a Field

What is that sound after rain? He says the corn is drinking, soil
sating itself with water. She sees uncountable tongues uncoil.

She finds the head of a rabbit. A fox, he says, stashed it
for lean days. At such bloody harvest, she can't help but recoil.

Crickets sing for sex, he tells her, sing with their knees.
She holds her legs straight in the sheets, beginning to recoil.

Winter arrives with Orion. He joins the hunters. Their orange backs
move slowly; they raise their rifles, bring home the spoil.

Green spears of squill (planted and forgotten) rise from cold
dirt, and from thrusting pistils and stamens, blue petals uncoil.

When the corn stands high, she walks barefoot across red soil,
a stranger to that house. A sinewy part of her begins to re-coil.

Laryngitis

The Fourth of July and I can't utter a word:
Can't call the doctor.
Can't call in to the radio call-in show.
Where's that freedom of speech now?

The tongue, so willing,
has been tasked with a beggar's trick:
Ask, ask, ask.
Before the hyoid bone clicked
into place in the pre-sapient throat,
rarefying howl and grunt,
food, drink, sex needed no discussion.
Now we must *ask*.

I declare freedom from speech,
my lips pure as the curve of Lady Liberty's.
Mute, I'll wear no sign,
carry a bell without a clapper,

open my mouth for food, drink, sex,
whatever waits on fork or glass
or lover's tongue or the unmediated air,
mouth clean as a hound's.

In the Middle of Things

We are fighting as we turn into the parking lot with a view of the lake, the lake going down to red clay with the August heat, the lake turning its back on the green shore against which it has happily spooned for months.

An eagle is lifting away from the backwater behind the marina, white tail flaring and white head, like paper flung from a window, like anything that makes our eyes cut, showing whites.

We are fighting about the usual, those things we fight about, and the eagle is carrying something long and limp, a snake or a water-soaked stick to add to the residence, beating black wings to gain altitude.

And if we were not fighting, I might have said, see, the eagle, and if you were not staring out the opposite window, you would have noticed.

Notorious

Need Press? Repeat: 'Green,' 'Sex,' 'Cancer,' 'Secret,' 'Fat'
— headline from *The New York Times*

It would become later, though not at first, a secret–
an affair worthy of a Restoration rake and a green
girl, all about the *sex sex sex*,
urgent, as though a diagnosis of cancer
had sent a shudder through the fat
of my frame, alarm bell tolling, no longer safe.

It had been one thing to feel safe
with him, to sigh after love like the Secret
after the Offertory—another to roll in the fat
of indulgence, to gourmandize until green
in the face, a real *Tropic of Cancer*
romp through a corn maze of sex,

itchy and hot and exhausting. No need to sex
up the story—middle-aged woman flees the safe
haven of post-marriage celibacy, the slow cancer
of a new old-maid-hood, virginity secreted
for reuse by matronly Hera at some green
bosky pool—too bad it's that *other* goddess considered phat

enough for contemporary tastes. I had dropped the fat
into the fire, breathing sizzle for substance, sex
as a refuge from that familiar green
goblin who rides the shoulder of a once-wife—now safe-
cracker, plunderer, other-woman. *His* secret
now become *my* secret, a karmic realignment of Cancer

and Scorpio, claws clacking. Isn't it true, after all, cancer
is just a crab, side-shifting, clutching the fat
chicken rump only to be reeled from the bay like a secret
agent summoned from the cold? In such late-season light, sex
appeal fades like a superannuated actor—wrinkles, age spots, safe
combing-over of hair—doomed to a perpetual green

room! Ludicrous, perhaps, to give the green
light to lust when straddling 50, when concerns should be cancer
prevention, glaucoma, pension—but I'd not be a woman safe
as the unsharpened edge of an implement, fat
as the fingers of an incurious man employed to sex
chickens, a known quantity, unsuspected of any deep dark secret.

In the safe review of the rearview mirror the affair wobbles away, fat
in the ass—anticlimactic as a colonoscopy sans cancer. Still, sex
kept a branch green in diminishing days. Now, finger to lips: "Secret!"

So This Is What You Wanted?

A drop of weak acid, to gnaw
atom from atom.

An unnamed stone, drawn
across the known, to mark or be marked.

A grinder to crush, a hammer to break,
heat that can melt, or worse, deep cold

until a word shatters.

Second Honeymoon

Moonlight on watered cobbles of Montorgueil:
limp endive, aging *coquilles*, cigarettes
bob down the gutter. "My feet," I plead, hobble
past *cave et boucherie*, Stohrer's *baguettes*.
We sleep among the great, on Marie-Stuart,
pres de where Madeleine drops her veils
to end as Saint-Denis, (yet after dark
aren't all cats gray, and lips alike, female
and male?) Our nights are loud and mornings rue-
full. Look—on this *place*—a severed head listens
for a loving word. I lean into the statue's
stony hand, and on command, I grin.
Late marriages, like poems, we revise,
but cannot step into the same street twice.

Dark Matter

Seaweed, scoured from the deep, scatters
its beads upon the beach. Everything broken.
I gather twists and bits, small lives blasted

and holed, shoved aside by the waves, a slattern's
house(un)keeping, fires heaped with trash,
any salutary offerings to one goddess or another

scrabbled up by dirty hands, a smidge and a smatter
to feed a momentary appetite. So I kick along the tide
line and analogize, my disappearing domestic

bliss no match for weighty issues of war-shatter
everywhere east to west, eruptions staggering the world;
but still, but still, I accumulate little bomblets

of disaster and embrace them, the spatter
of heartsblood ready to fly when the least jounce
lets it all come apart, and so the personal

etc. holds little hands with the larger all the way up, dark matter
flinging this fine universe outward from one hot bang,
farther, colder, the space-between we imagine.

4
Scorch

Alienation

Sometimes he almost
knows: His diaphragm
sore from breathing too deeply,

thighs trembling after that visitor
from other space, remote
except when his body

bucks impossibly to meet
the infinitely desirable,
deep eyes from beyond

Andromeda, uncanny curves
of skull, shoulder.
He wakes, remembering

blind light. He moves
through the house, touching
tender spots along his ribs,

his probed body and sectioned heart.
In the kitchen, he eats
cold spaghetti while standing at the fridge,

then draws water, letting it run
as he strokes the satisfying chrome
of the faucet. His wife is on the phone:

He stands at the door,
watching as her chubby hands
gesture, fall flat to the couch.

She takes up her knitting,
her face blue in the light of the TV.
She wants nothing

else, nothing but this:
A whisper from the black leech
riding her brain stem.

On the Beach

> *We came upon shells, mounds of shells, many ancient and weathered and gleaming white against the white-gray sand.*
> —Edwin Way Teale, from *North with the Spring*, "Seashell Islands"

So many, such lives:
oysters relentlessly seining
the sea, mussels too,
draining the insubstantial, parting
the water from the waters,
scallops improbably hunting
on jet drive, oyster drills
drilling, whelks inserting
a toothed foot into the soft
flesh of their brethren, coquinas
rolling out of Carolina sand
with each wave
and furiously reburying,
in such numbers that even with flesh
tiny as baby's fingernail,
the multitudes, aggregated,
would boil into a hearty broth.

Such onetime lives:
carbonate castles
knitted up from the waves,
emptied, become home
to hermit crabs
trying on the concavities
of the columella
into which their soft abdomens
like size-10 derrieres in size-8 jeans
are snuggled—
sometimes a wholesale
resettlement,
the largest, finding a
greater gastropod,
moving on up, and the next
taking his former abode,

down to the least
and miserable clinger
to a sponge or a worm shell
now claiming a tiny palace.

The shells of bivalves, too,
housing multitudes,
first resting-place
of coral and barnacle,
kelp and sea urchins,
oyster fry putting down
roots on the half-shells
that, storm-loosened,
tumble whitely onto the beach
for the collectors.

Eventually,
eight-fingered tourists
will pick up a skull in the wreck of a city,
shake off the gray regolith
(which they will taste, *must* taste)
polish the zygomatic arch,
listen for the surf pounding
at the eyeholes.
What beautiful remains!
Each one alike yet different,
thousands and millions
shaped for beauty alone:
consider the knitting of the fissures,
the curve of the dome.

Stratigraphy

In archaeological sites, natural and human-generated materials occur together in layers. These layers, called strata, form a record of past events...
—Research Laboratories of Archaeology, UNC

Prehistory
is what has been cut apart
and swallowed,
bite by terrible bite,
and laid down in the body's lattice.
Small sharp things:
that glance across the table,
those unfinished gestures.

History waits in the antechamber
for the arrival of words:
no documents, no history.
But what's down inside
the long galleries of the bones
all the while, without any light,
painting aurochs on the walls?

Now if you only want to pry
artifacts out of the generations
of mud, what can be salvaged
for love or for money,
hurry, then, with pick and shovel—
difficult to tell what it all
amounted to, once,
except that sometimes
in the upended clay the light
finds a carved head, a bit of gold,
or flaked edge of obsidian
that might (or not) have been employed
in a clenched fist.

The careful investigator,
with dental pick and bone brush,
would find the same shattered femurs,

the same engraved figures
(vulva and tectiform shelter),
but frame them
in time and meaning:
how high the icy water rose
that spring,
how the deer fled,
how we starved.

Out of the Ordinary

My friend mourns the missing thrushes,
ee-o-lay that used to rise
like fireflies at the verge of oak woods.

Her memory saves a space for their song;
others, later, won't notice the lack,
satisfied by the insistent mockingbird

(his repertoire a hundred songs or more,
including cell phone and cricket chirp),
reweaving a looser web of dawn chorus:

So one bird replaces a canopy of absent
warblers, as a synthesizer sets ghosts
in the chairs of an emptied orchestra.

❧

Like the scissored silhouette
of a child's shadow, this becomes the *is*
of what *isn't*. What is *no longer*,

like those ballads that bridged generations.
We no longer lift our quotidian voices
to pace work or ease the idle hours,

now that professionals provide
tunes at the ready, electronically
clipped and smoothed,

like purebred stock at the fair,
not one hair out of place,
not one note quavered.

Choice of Words

My father and I
each became single
in the same year.

He is *bereft*,
robbed of his happiness,
a *widower*, or *widowman*.

His life has come undone,
and he is adrift
among the wreckage.

The only words worthy
of his loss are Anglo-Saxon
uncensored howls.

But I am *separated*
on the way to *divorce*,

terms for a civilized
coming apart.

Separated like an egg,
occasionally messy

but with some care
the yolk rests aloft,

while the white goes
cool and sliding into the bowl.

In plain words,
it's all butchery,

whatever the parting:
disjointed, sundered, severed.

A separation is also,
however, embarkation.

We stand at the rail,
each waving a white handkerchief
at the sinking shore.

Watch the Sun Come Up on Your Own Life

The nature of the tourist
is that she has nothing to do

despite the itineraries,
no place to settle.

It's all about glutting
the eyes, nose, ears,

sucking in all this
foreignness, even

the diesel exhaust
along famous boulevards

where one glance
up would present her

with a mother scrubbing
a child's neck, a youth

naked from the shower,
an old man inspecting

a worrisome mole—
moments when light

reaches deeply into familiar
rooms and we pay heed

to our dutiful bodies
newly not the same.

Work in the Morning

Two branches need to come off the red cedar:
the first one springy, sparse, raggedly
alive but angled like a badly set bone, the other
a stub long dry and weather-polished.
The bow saw is wide at the base to take a solid shove,
narrowing to nudge into tight junctures. Push, pull,
the living branch spills a runnel of sawdust;
the wood shows white with a small red heart.

The stub offers smooth gray skin and cinnabar dust—
seasoned in summer and winter, it does not yield easily.
Hard work in the shoulder, hard work in the back,
here I am doing woodsman's labor as I have before,
slower at the sawing and stacking, but enough of that: The reward
sufficient in the sharp whiff, the satisfying crack
of stub from stump, saw-polished, dark red across all its rings.

I stop at the back door—isn't there some other chore to do, outside?
That darkened room is every day more familiar,
the worn-out body on the couch, curled like a wood shaving,
(long-drawing-out, the measure and measure and slow measure
toward that *snick*), her breath pulled in like a burdened rope,
breath by breath drawing us tightly into the same coil.
I lean the saw against the step. Sun refracts
from the bright, honed teeth, specific for their work of parting.

In War

1

*Whump whump
whump.
Whump whump whump.*

I think, *it's thunder,*
but those high white cumulus,
(fat merchanters, sails
full as they make way east),
bear no threat of storm.

Ragged groups of three,
*whump
whump whump.*

Miles away across
the sun-soaked piney woods,
young artillerymen
at Fort Bragg
attend to their studies.

2

My father talks
about artillery *walking*,
how the shells soared
over their heads
and burst on the enemy,

the men laboring over
newly shattered ground, trusting
the skill of their artillerymen,
that the covering fire
would move steadily forward,

that a shell
would not drop
short.

This firing
comes no closer,
but I am easier
when I turn
up the hill and away.

3

Whump
whump whump.
When shells light
among the Carolina pines,
pitch flares.

Trunks char,
briers and filth
burn clean,
and new grass
springs.

I've walked in blackened
woods to view the unforeseen
result of artillery practice;
because fire is left to burn
among the longleaf pines,

tiny woodpeckers,
(martial in black uniforms
with red cockades)
have returned, satisfied
by scorched earth beneath their nests.

4

The creek is so small
at Antietam, a trickle.
There is this bridge, and farm lane,
and unremarkable patches
of oaks and maples.

"Artillery Hell," they called it,
five hundred cannons, firing
down upon the fields,
cross-hatching the regiments,
cutting the summer corn

"as closely as could
have been done with a knife,
and the slain laid in rows
precisely as they stood
in their ranks."

Silence thumbs into
my head, the pressure
of a shocked atmosphere,
or the quiet
after drums have burst.

Losing Ground

DUNKARD MILL RUN, WEST VIRGINIA: THE FARM

1

Forest once-upon-a.
Deer chestnut turkey bear ginseng oak squirrel berry. Once.
Then saws and axes made great trees human-size.
Cabin into house, scratched plot to fields, to industrial
drifts of hogs battening on the trash of hotel kitchens.
Later, the ground was in hay. Timothy and foxtail.
Wind stroked the hill's long flanks.

2

We built a house and made a new garden:
bowls and bones came up with each shovel turn.
I grew corn and cantaloupe, beans and tomatoes.
Dug deep to plant orchards, though
not deep enough to root the marriage.

3

The first year, stunned by loneliness,
I planted but didn't tend.
The next summer, volunteer tomatoes
struggled against pigweed. By the time
witchgrass overran the strawberries
and the raspberries crumbled from virus,
I was gone, too.

4

I expect my apples still bear faithfully:
Lodi Macoun Spy and Winesap.
Asparagus will last decades,
but apples are for generations.
Until forest.

Greensboro, North Carolina: The Women

Snowdene lived all her married years and then her widowed years in the little white house on Elam. She planted spider lilies, four o'clocks, Spanish bells, snow on the mountain. When she put down her trowel, I came along to pick it up. Finding, freeing, lifting and replanting, I was Bingham at Machu Picchu, Carter in Egypt, rediscovering the old.

I planted irises brought from West Virginia: yellow flags from a swale on the farm, bronze giants whose knotty rhizomes had been passed to me by a mountain woman. I planted lilies of the valley that my mother had carried from state to state to state.

One day, on a cut-across street, I saw a sign by a cottage: "Ditch lilies, dig all you want." An old woman sat on the porch as I lifted clumps of orange trumpets. All you want, she said. With years of growth and spread, they had choked themselves and needed new ground.

In the summer sun I spaded up baskets of lilies to plant on Elam, where I lived solitary and then lived married at that little white house.

LEAWOOD DRIVE: LILIES

      1

Did they survive our December move?

      2

I waited for spring.
Double River Wye spiked up
and blossomed, along with nameless
others, white, mango, golden-throat, grape.
Year by year I set out new additions:
Children's Festival, Coney Island, Old King Cole.
The last I planted were lemon lilies,
Hemerocallis flava, fragrant sister
to those hoyden ditch lilies.

      3

June 5.
I backed down the driveway.
White Orientals trumpeted
by the mailbox, and Happy Returns shone
with sunny promises not to be kept.

      4

Each night at the edge of uneasy sleep,
I imagined the unfolding show—
blossoms opening and fading
without my witness,
still, I know how the lilies increase,
roots fattening in the clay.

SOMEWHERE TO GO

Attachment is the cause of pain, but then, the Buddha was no gardener.

From Leawood I took what could be carried: a red rose in a green pot, a basket of strawberries. The scrabbly burr-rose from Elam, lifted yet again, roots (for a time) in sandy soil at my parents' home.

I cannot let go.

Not of any, not of a life lived by growing and tending. Not of the lilies of the valley moved and moved, not of the silvery money plant, seeded and reseeded. Not the lilies, not the iris, not the striped camellia I blessed each morning. Not even the pink phlox straggling beside the road where once I stood to catch the school bus. Even that.

I fly home and home and home.

5
MUCK

Lore

Trust water only from springs:
Creeks and rivers murmur of white quartz,
willow shade, minnows flashing silver sides—
dissembling the doe, dead upstream from a misspent bullet.

Place no hands where eyes haven't been:
A rock ledge on a warm March morning
crawls with snakes knotted around nothing
but the expectation of an open palm.

Douse a fire twice, then cover with dirt:
One ember can smolder a resinous root
to flame that runs the ground to bedded leaves, spruce
boughs, trunks fingering fire straight to the sky.

Carry it in full, take it out empty:
But mistakes, hollow as bottles, get heavier
the longer they are carried, the farther
you try to haul them.

Catechism

Quickly!
Before your memory fades—
what did you see?
        Grass moving in the wind, birds, young pines
        like bottlebrushes, squirrels.
No, no, you must
remember better—
what did you see?
        Bull nettle sharp with glassy needles,
        partridge berry,
        Venus' looking-glass in endless self-reflection.
Good, good.
        And persimmon blossoms
        scattered like confetti, sassafras.
        White-tailed deer, a herd
        divided by my presence.
        Mockingbirds, towhees,
        fetterbush, poison oak, grape.
What grape?
        Muscadine, I guess.
Or scuppernong?
        And butterflies in the deep woods
        like flying shadows. Swallowtails.
Pipevine? Spicebush?
        I do not know.
        Some kind of peaflower, I remember, white and pink.
        Some kind of oak, the leaves rounded. White oak.
But what about the smallest,
the shrinking and timid and camouflaged?
        Those I didn't see.
Not the jewel-backed beetles
nor the worms in the galls
nor the agaric just starting to swell
nor the small herbs among the grasses
nor the voles in the pine straw?

        No. But I can tally
        meadow rue and dewberry,
        a fox squirrel black as burned pine trunks,
        a blue-tailed skink, pipsissewa.

But did you see Eustis Lake Beard Tongue,
(it should be in blossom now, pink blossom)
or trailing arbutus,
or painted buntings?
        No.
Not the buntings?
        No. None.

Then they are gone.

What you see, that is what survives.
What you remember is all there is.

Don't you want to save the world?

Spandrel

I wake up with a word on my tongue:
spandrel.
No dictionary here, I let the syllables
roll back and forth with the rocking
of the boat, span-drel, span-drel.

I delve among rhymes—wastrel,
who spends his legacy and falls among swine;
a scoundrel, taking away the loot;
a mongrel, houseless, fawning for a meal.
All diminutives, all shabby lives.

Spandrel, I will say,
is a maker of bridges,
as the minstrel is a maker of songs.

I see him carry in a leather bag
his mallet, saw, bit and brace,
walking ahead of,
but never beyond,
some history.

With materials at hand—
washed stone, oak, pitch pine—
he joins bank to bank, life to life,
across streams too difficult to ford,
not worth a ferry.

Each blow of wood on wood
sets ripples on the water:
deo gratias, deo gratias.

The Guide: Cave Paintings at Font de Gaume

Here are the bison—
two, three, four—see
as I move my light along the wall,
the head, the back, the legs.

I come with these prepared words
for the tourists, allowed for 30 minutes
to breathe the same air as the cave,
to shuffle along the permitted path,
to look at what I can show them,
and sometimes they see.

Always, they notice the graffiti.
Their eyes are drawn to it,
cut into the limestone, even into the animals,
names and dates from the time of revolutions,
the time of kings, and marks made by those
who can only mark, letterless peasants
bent always to the soil.

Ignore those childish scratchings,
please. See the mammoth, here,
the auroch's curving horns.
So long ago, yet those artists understood
perspective; this leg is clearly behind that one.
How long until we learned that again?
Centuries.

Shadow creates the animals
as much as iron and black manganese:
the artists employing the shape of the stone
and the moving flames to give life.
After the artists,
the animals waited
in full darkness, in quietude,
until men would return with torches.

I wave my light along the line of the herd,
knowing how it begins—
a shoulder juts, a hoof shifts,
and the herd rolls forward.
I see tears on one woman's face
like water on the walls.

My grandfather was one of those
boys who knew the cave, who came
with candles and lanterns
and (being boys) *toujours de l'audace*,
going into the earth, the twisting
humid blackness.
No guide, then, no electric bulbs along the floor,
and the broad day when they had scrabbled
into the mountain
disappeared after two turns.

Narrow passages, but not so tight
for slender boys.
They made jokes and noises
and pushed each other into crevices,
against the seeping walls.
They lifted their lamps to see
a reindeer licking the head of another,
a horse, its ribs swelling.
It breathed in, out.
Les bêtes, les bêtes,
walking beside them, deeper into the cave,
toward secrets always just past
the circle of their light, where
stone comes down too close
to crawl any farther.

Stone swallowed their eagerness,
no matter how loudly they shouted,
and then, because the immemorial
darkness had taken their voices,
they pulled small knives
from their pockets and they cut:

We were here.
We saw.
We felt the animals rise inside us
until we did not know ourselves.

Racial Memory

I'm falling out of a tree
I'm falling out of a tree
I'm falling

       With one foot on the sailboat transom,
         I'm kicking the rudder down, but it slips,
again, bobs to the surface,
and I extend (just a little, a little more)
when my foot slides and I'm

Falling out of a tree
Falling

       I have fifty feet of Lake Kerr
        under my ass, but instead of pushing
         off the boat and plashing, I cling,
slide, slice two claw-marks down my shin
and smack a shiner on my knee.

Help me, help me
I'm falling out of the tree

       Baby in the cradle in the tree-top,
last thought, night after night
flung from sleep by the *falling*,
out of safety, out of the branches,
knowing only *lion, leopard, lion, leopard*,

jerking upright in bed, thudding pulse
and a last good breath, as though falling asleep
were any more dangerous
than arcing backward into lake water
black with the dreams of drowned forests.

Old Story

1

At the edge of Appalachian forests,
dogwood testifies: rusty print of nails
on white cruciform petals,
a crown of thorns.

Expert at finding patterns,
we spot sacredness
in passionflower and lotus,
golden apples and golden bough.

Even the bleached bodies
of sand dollars offer a dole of grace:
number the wounds, count the stars,
and angels spilling from the broken whole.

2

So this man wearing a Snap-on Tools cap
tells me that he was alone in Galveston,
alone on the beach among storm-driven voices,
his life misplaced, mishandled, mistaken,

when he came upon the desiccated head
of a giant catfish. Turning it over,
he peered into the raw gape—
and what he saw sent him spinning homeward,

a crucified Christ enshrined,
face inclined, flayed arms forever pinioned.

Lore II: Tap's Tips

Lost, you can follow water down
to civilization—a bridge, a mill, a town—because
water makes wealth.

Dry leaves are a comforter
for the forlorn—tunneled into, they trap heat
and life. In snow country, hemlock boughs
bent over your single bed may be sealed by snowfall.

You can daub your shoes with mink oil,
waterproof your coat
and hat, dip matches in paraffin
and seal them in a tube.

But not having planned to enter the trail,
nor to lose it,
you have made no provision.
No matches, no hook, no coil of line, no knife.

You eat what the season allows: fiddleheads,
the pith of cattails, cress, dandelion greens,
morels if they are not false, strawberries,
blackberries, blueberries, fox grapes,

feral apples, hickory nuts, walnuts, Indian potatoes,
bird eggs, turtle eggs, frogs, dace, crayfish,
a nest of hairless mice,
yellow clay, clean snow, a pane of ice.

Remember:
Honey cleanses wounds
but so do maggots.

Consider that the ones who love you
will not look long enough.

Occam's Razor

Furtive bird
belly deep in bog,
careful wader, frog fishing
the aperture between swamp
and the undershade of trees:
a king rail?

On closer encounter,
dagger beak, slaty back;
a skeptical yellow eye
blinks, the neck stretches
longer than expected
and the rail reshapes
to a green heron,
no more exotic here than me.

I crumple my checklist:
Do not multiply
birds beyond necessity.

Last Sweet

Not like early summer
juice bursting under thin skin Candor
peaches dawning in pecks
and half-bushels along Route 220,

or Redhaven, Winblo, and Ellerbe
swelled to a swagger
with midsummer drowse
of cicada and honeysuckle:

Fall peaches have grown slowly
under a shortened sun,
and duskier shadows drape
the shoulders of Carolina Belle,

mellowing outward from the pit,
the flesh grown close
into a furrowed pericardium, scarlet
and sweet at its vitals.

Given Half a Chance

The Autumn Glory sedum failed to redden,
planted too deep in shade;

what light's let in by the shedding
maple is too late, too thin.

Now what made the summer garden
will have to stay: lank lilies, massed ranks

of Marvel-of-Peru, sundrops overrun
by roses, chance plants from the farmers' market

not always true to name. Late sun
pushes long shadows across the garden:

what's too deep-rooted, mis-chosen,
invasive, choked or choking

must stay for winter,
no more planting, now,

no more lifting or dividing.
Still, this afternoon

through blowing leaves, I carried home
a willow in a bucket.

6
Evoke

A Blessing on the Tongue

1. Farmer's Market

Big as a softball/a cat's head/a clay clod
turned up in wet plowing, apples to give pause,
KING LUST scratched in black marker
on the lip of the cardboard box.

Old apples, these, without the Irish setter
gleam of Gala, the narrow hips of Red Delicious.
A ragged mantle of red covers the yellow
shoulders, skin pocked with lenticels.

I buy three, filling a bag,
and eat one as I drive. Sweet and rich,
the juice coats my hand, an apple in full,
an apple in spate.

2. KING LUST

Imagine:
Henry VIII tossing Francis in a wrestling match
for a prize basket of these apples,
filling his doublet with them for walks at Hampton Court,
and when painted by Holbein, he held this
fat apple in his fist,
(painted over later with a chivalric glove
as the apple was deemed too ripe a symbol.)

King Lust:
Ahasuerus decrees: *Let Queen Vashti*
come before me, wearing only
her royal crown,
to show the nations and ministers her beauty.
The queen would not be summoned
so Esther stoops to conquer.

King Lust:
Crowned desire, the king
choosing this one or that,
David and Bathsheba, Anne Boleyn,
Madame de Pompadour,
Nell Gwyn, Lola Montez,
Edward and Wallis …

King Lust:
An apple the size of a girl's breast/
a jeweled hilt/a crown/
an empire.

3. By An(y) Other Name: King Lush

LUSH is an **object-oriented**
programming **language** for researchers
interested in large-scale
numerical and **graphic applications.**
LUSH is designed **to be used**
to combine the flexibility
of a **high-level**, weakly-typed
language, **with the** efficiency
of a **natively-compiled** language.

>From Middle English, *lusch*, soft, tender.
The sort to become easily
intoxicated, in English English
a supple flirt—
all over my man after just one pint!
yet desirable.
In American, a stumblebum,
red-nosed, reeking of booze,
mashing his words into a stew.

The adjective "lush," which can
      sometimes
mean
"delicious" as well,
      is not a shortened form of "luscious";
it derived
      on its own.

Merriam-Webster

4. The Arrival of King Luscious

A young farmer,
round-cheeked like his mountain apples,
arrays his crop: Gala, Grimes, Delicious,
King Luscious.

The King's birth is clouded,
arriving by chance
in the throes of the Depression,
a foundling from Hendersonville, NC.

Some look to his heft
and say he's no by-blow,
mere accident of the orchard,
but claim him as the natural child
of Stayman and Wolf River.

A small tree
but rich in fruit,
late to the harvest,
needing frost.

5. King Luscious

> *Lucius, king of the Britons, sent to Pope Eleutherius, thirteenth in succession from St. Peter, to entreat that he would dispel the darkness of Britain by the light of Christian instruction. This surely was the commendable deed of a magnanimous prince....*
> —William of Malmesbury

Here's to Lucius, later saint, name and provenance in doubt,
a small lord in Switzerland, most like, never England's king,

the error of a holy inksman nodding at his vellum, worn out
with the Word. Not so great a leap, then, to King Luscious,

canonized for the apples gilding his orchard, as Brigid
was for amber beer miraculously brewed from her bathwater:

"I should like a great *lake* of beer for the King of Kings...
through all Eternity to see Heaven's family drinking."

The good king died "without heir," say the annals, nonetheless,
we'll treasure his yellow apple of indifferent demeanor

but good heart. Bless apples full of Sun, bursting their skins,
cool from the branch, warm off the hearth, juice running over!

Raise a basket, a bushel, or a peck to honor his chilly feast.
Take and eat, let this sweet flesh melt into savor.

You Don't Leave It on the Side of the Road

Only the skunk
(who is precious in the sight
of the Almighty,
for his first-fingers marked its back
like you'd stroke a cat's)—

that piss-kitty
just humping across the road
headed for what egg-breaking
or cricket hunting
it does in the night—

when the tire finds it and the wheel,
(the bump too small to be a body
broken but it was), raises up
a smell from earth to heaven
like a mortal soul

clinched for the longest time
to the ankle of its death.

Valerie Nieman's poems have appeared widely and been collected in two chapbooks and her debut collection, *Wake Wake Wake* (Press 53). She has held writing fellowships from the National Endowment for the Arts and the North Carolina Arts Council. Her books of prose include three novels, with the most recent, *Blood Clay*, being honored with the Eric Hoffer Award. She is a graduate of West Virginia University and Queens University of Charlotte. A professor of creative writing at North Carolina A&T State University, she teaches at John Campbell Folk School and other venues, and serves as poetry editor for *Prime Number Magazine*. You may encounter her on a train, or solo hiking, or over a cup of lemon-ginger tea at a local bookstore.

About the Cover Artist

Marko Nadj lives in Sombor, a city in the northern part of Serbia, where he goes to medical school. He discovered his passion for photography in 2011 at the age of 13. He says, "At the beginning, photography was only for fun, but as time passed I started to think about the meaning of my photographs as well as the message they sent to viewers." Marko says he enjoys creating dark photographs, although they don't have much in common with his personal life. He describes his work as poetic and mystical, and he likes heavily edited photos with a lot of textures. He also enjoys self portraits because they enable him to connect deeper with the characters he creates. He hopes that his story will prove to the world that art is available to people of all ages. You can find more of Marko's photography on Facebook and Flickr.

www.ingramcontent.com/pod-product-compliance
Lightning Source LLC
LaVergne TN
LVHW041342080426
835512LV00006B/584